The Writer's Block Survival Guide

101 First Lines to Help You Start Writing the Great American Novel

Webster House Publishing LLC
Ridgefield, Connecticut

Cover and Interior Design by Linda Robinson

Copyright ©2012 by Webster House Publishing LLC. All rights reserved. No part of this book, including interior design, cover design, and icons, may be reproduced or transmitted in any form, by any means (electronic, photocopying, recording, or otherwise) without the prior written permission of the publisher.

ISBN-10: 1-932635-33-5
ISBN-13: 978-1-932635-33-1

Printed in the United States of America

10 9 8 7 6 5 4 3 2 1

For additional information about Webster House Publishing LLC titles or Get Smart Book® book titles, contact us on the Internet at
http://*www.websterhousepub.com* or write to
Webster House Publishing LLC, Box 294, Georgetown, CT 06829

NOTICE: If anyone chooses to use any of these first lines in their own work, we cannot be responsible for the results, unless, however, it meets with great success. Then we would appreciate a small percentage of your royalties, and although it is not a requirement of using this book, it would certainly be most welcome (although unexpected).

INTRODUCTION

Imagine opening a book and it began with, "Day one; there was nothing around, but God decided to fix that." It just doesn't have the same punch as "In the beginning God created the heavens and the earth," which is considered the most famous first line. Or think about an editor with a stack of manuscripts piled on her desk. The first line of the manuscript she picks up reads, "I'm a young sailor named Ishmael." I think the first response would be, "Who cares?" But if it starts off with "Call me Ishmael" there's something about it that grabs you. It's terse, it's demanding, and it catches your attention.

Often the first opening line of a novel or story is the grabber, and if that doesn't do the trick, your long labored-over book may possibly hit the reject pile. That's why we've compiled this list of first lines. Herein you'll find 101 interesting (we think) opening salvos for your book, depending on the subject matter. There's some Romance, some Science Fiction, Mysteries, and so on—something for everyone. You may like some of them enough to use them, perhaps in an altered form. We've even given you blank pages with each opening line so that you can start writing.

More important, these will give you some practice in starting your long-awaited book. Frankly, it's hard to write a good book or story. Titles are easier. We had a friend who had a notebook full of great titles for his unwritten novels. Each title was better than the last, but alas, there was no book forthcoming. When asked why he hadn't begun any of these books, his response was "I just can't get started." And that's the problem.

INTRODUCTION *(continued)*

Pick any of the opening lines in this book and start writing. Even if you do nothing with it, it's good practice. Feel free to change "him" to "her" and proper names to protect the innocent. These are "starter" lines and make whatever alterations work for you.

It is said that Ernest Hemingway usually stopped writing in the middle of a paragraph so that when he went back to work the next day, he could continue with the ideas that he'd already begun, and continue on from there. Again, getting started is half the battle.

We're already planning Volume 2 (or II, depending on how fancy we plan to get), and we would love to receive ideas from our readers. Fill in the form at the back of this book and mail it to us. If we publish it in the next edition, we'll certainly mention your name (if you wish). Or you can email your first lines to us at *info@websterhousepub.com*. Please indicate "First Lines" in the subject so it won't go into spam.

Enjoy the book.

Part I

101 First Lines to Help You Start
Writing the Great American Novel

Once upon a time. . .

The sun was shining when I stepped outside.

Rain pelted me as I hurried through the streets to meet with him (her).

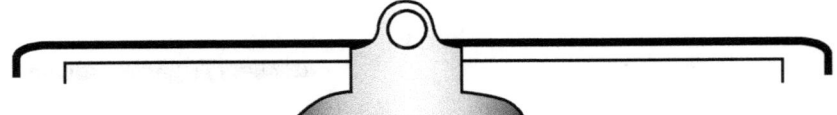

Bzzz. The cellphone vibrated in his pocket. He knew who it was and was loathe to answer it.

Wham! The first blow caught me on the side of my head. The room began to spin.

When she walked into the room, everyone held their collective breath.

I poured myself a cup of coffee, opened the paper, and prepared myself for a day of relaxation. How was I to know it would be over in less time than it took to finish my coffee?

I was born in a small town in the south, but I left shortly after my 18th birthday.

Harry had never been late for anything in his life, so when he failed to show up for our weekly dinner, I knew he was in trouble.

As we approached the sailboat, we could see that there was no one aboard.

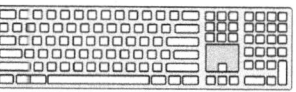

At the first cough of the engine, I knew it was going to mean trouble.

They say you can't go home again, but I had to try. Resolution would be my only salvation.

My parents always admonished me, "Don't be afraid of the dark," but I doubt that either of them had been in this place before.

I can't say enough about _____. Until I met him, my life had been one of unending boredom.

"I want a divorce" was the first thing she said when I answered the phone.

He stood in the alleyway across the street, watching with amusement as the police rushed up the stairs of the building he had left five minutes earlier. He knew what they were going to find.

There are good days, there are bad days. When she walked into my office, I knew this was going to be a good day.

"Oh my God," she screamed as the lottery numbers flashed on the screen. From that moment on, our lives would be changed forever.

"Once I tell you this secret," she said, "you'll never be the same again." I could have walked away, but I didn't. She was right.

-

-

-

The radio was blaring, the kids in the back were arguing about the umpire's bad call, and I didn't see the stop sign.

When we first brought Charlie home from the kennel, he was three months old with the sweetest face you ever saw. Little did we know what we were in for.

It had been six months since he came to this tiny island. Most of the pain was now behind him. She would always be a piece of him, but it was time to move ahead. But how?

She knew today was to be the last day of her life, as she carried the deadly burden strapped to her body, into the crowded bus terminal. She was unafraid.

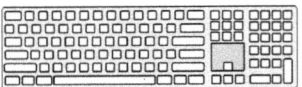

She always believed that one day her prince would come. And here he was, standing right in front of her. She was glad she came to the party. Life was about to change.

"I'm leaving," she said.

It has been fifteen years since I had heard her voice. "She's dead," was all she said.

As soon as I cut the red wire, I knew I had made a fatal mistake.

The new fallen leaves crackled and snapped beneath my feet as I walked up the Dean's front path. Why had he called me?

The president shook his head over my weak objections. "You're my guy," he said, "and I want you to take care of this quickly, quietly—and permanently."

When she opened her eyes and saw him sleeping next to her, she realized it had not been a dream. It was really him!

There was a lot riding on the next shot. A lot? Hell, my entire life depended on making it.

I am not the most reliable person when it comes to making plans.

"Strange," she thought as she reentered the room. "Hadn't there been a woman's scarf on the back of the chair just moments before?"

It was a Sunday morning, a day filled with promise. It ended with threats.

"Cease fire," someone yelled to our left, and silence slowly enveloped us as we lay in the gully. We could hear the cries of the wounded, from both our comrades and the enemy, somewhere in the field ahead.

There is an enormous burden lifted from your shoulders once you've determined that this day would be your last.

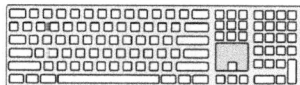

Ryan fell back onto the couch, so overwhelmed by her passion, that he did not notice when three other dark-robed people entered the room behind them.

He had promised himself that that this was to be his last time.

Today I am fifteen.

As the shouting grew closer, my lungs bursting with agony, I regretted the years of cigarettes, vodka, and broken promises to myself to go to the gym.

When he woke up that morning, he knew that this would be a very special day, just like his parents had promised.

Despite being wet and dirty, it seemed to me that the big yellow dog that stood on our doorstep seemed to be smiling.

My first book was a modest success, my second a complete failure. Yet, this latest oeuvre was destined to be a best seller, and would change my life completely.

"You were yelling in your sleep," my wife said, shaking me gently. "Who's Clöe?"

"Wow," I thought. "This was going to be better than I ever imagined."

Despite the fact that my eyes were starting to close, I knew I had to push on.

The first time I had seen a dead body was when my grandfather died when I was eight years old. The next time was this morning, fourteen years later, when we came across the three dead Iraqi solders lying beside their truck.

She was happy. I was not. "There's something missing here," I thought.

The moon floated just above the horizon. It was cold. And then the snow began. There was no hope now of finding him.

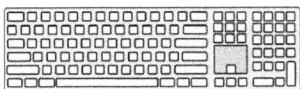

Many people do not believe in love at first sight. They're wrong.

When Earth's second moon was discovered, it excited the world. That excitement would soon turn to terror.

I don't care what the doctors have told me.
I plan on living another 25 years.

Connie lay in bed, tossing and turning, as she listened to her roommate and her boyfriend going at it in the bedroom next door.

Even though I was expecting it, when the phone rang, I almost dropped my drink.

Did you ever have one of those days when absolutely nothing goes right (wrong)?

The day my mother died was the last day my life was what one would call normal.

Every day the 7:45 a.m. train. The cup of black coffee (two sugars, no milk) when I disembarked at Grand Central Station. The short walk to my office. The elevator ride to the 22nd floor. Every day the same thing. Something had to change.

Trust me; you're going to have a hard time believing what I tell you.

When I saw her walking down the aisle toward me, as beautiful as she was, I knew at that moment this was going to be one of the worst mistakes of my life.

My name is _____ and I am an alcoholic.

When Susan awoke on Monday morning, she had a pulsating headache, and her body felt as if her blood was boiling. She didn't know it, but it was.

"I'm going to take you back before the accident," the hypnotist said, in a soft, droning voice.

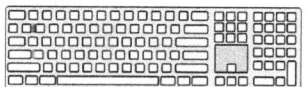

It began as a little icon in the upper left corner of everyone's browser, regardless of what URL you were browsing. And then it grew.

The face on the television was decidedly Slavic, but the accent was indeterminate. However, it was impossible to miss the activity that was being shown live, behind him as he addressed the cameras.

"Grandma," the boy cried. "Come out to the backyard to see what I've found."

He had just turned off the alarm for the store when he sensed a movement behind him. The next thing he knew he was flying forward onto the floor and recognized the unmistakable click of a weapon being cocked.

They had predicted the mother of all storms and they were right. It was going to make landfall at 2 in the morning and we knew we had to get out fast.

John Smith slowly drained the last of his Grey Goose Le Citron martini, stood up from the barstool, brushed his slacks carefully to smooth down the front, and left the bar. It was time.

"Oh my God" they both seemed to cry at the same time, and God must have been listening. They both lay back on the down pillows with satisfied smiles on their faces.

When the digital display on his phone told him it was his mother calling again, he grabbed his keys, threw on a jacket, and called the dog. "Come on, Charlie, let's go to the park." Enough was enough.

I'd been struggling to write the first line of my novel. I'd already worked out the title and the plot.

"Guilty!"

"Not guilty!"

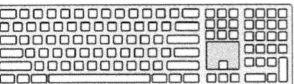

When I awoke that morning, I could hear the crowds shouting in the streets. The time had come.

The overture ended, the curtain rose, and as the lights slowly came up, the audience gasped in horror.

The first alert I had was the sound of horses growing restless. They knew something was coming.

When Phillip was nine years old, he discovered the secret trapdoor. He had been looking for the new litter of kittens Grandpa had told them was in the barn.

"Work with me," he yelled, as Andrea, dangling precariously from the rope, began to scream.

"Mayday, mayday," he shouted into the radio, as the small craft was tossed over and over again by the huge waves. Then he heard a slow, painful crack coming from the mast

Melinda and George stared in horror at the oncoming truck, swerving from lane to lane, completely out of control.

Betsy Holliday knew she looked good that morning as she got on the school bus.

The iPod was blasting in his ears, so he didn't hear his father enter the room. But he did see his father's face, and he felt his heart stop.

She was the one person I never expected to see in a place like this.

He was big. Bigger than anyone I had ever seen before. And he was coming straight toward me.

-
-
-

My eyes were dry but my heart was hammering in my chest as he turned, gave me a little smile, and walked out the door.

As she opened the door, she knew it had been a mistake. It was the first of many she would make that day.

The screen flickered as the president's face came into focus. He looked drawn. Behind him you could see the soldiers gathering in the streets.

If I have to tell you one more time to clean your room, there's no going to the circus tonight.

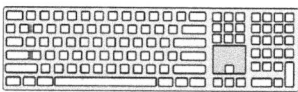

"I'm finally going to make the club," I thought, as she squeezed into the plane's tiny bathroom with me.

Before I begin, there are a few things you should know about me.

I should have worn my gun. My badge wasn't going to do it for me in that hell hole.

Trouble. Sometimes you can see it coming a long way off. And sometimes, like today, you're just too blind to see it if it pops up in front of you carrying a sign.

It doesn't matter how far you run, how deep you hide—if they want to find you, they will.

When she found her husband holding court in the den with three younger women, she could see that he was already passed his drink limit. It was going to be hell, again, when they got home.

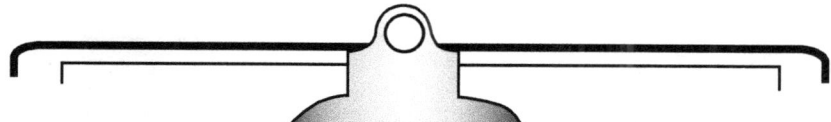

From the back of the bleachers it's sometimes hard to see what's going on at home plate. So when I heard the crack of the bat, the crowd beginning to roar, saw my father start to rise, I thought, "Oh my God, that ball is heading straight for us."

You can either love technology or you can hate it. Usually I loved it, but at this moment, as my cell began to play "Margaritaville" just as the conductor was tapping his baton to begin, I wanted to crawl under my seat.

My mother shook me gently awake. "Time to get dressed," she said. Today was my first day in the new school.

Let me tell you right off the bat, that there is a terrific advantage to being a dog. You can listen in on what people are saying, and if you pay attention, you can actually start to understand it, and nobody cares that you're eavesdropping, least of all my owner, the President of the United States.

As we drove up to the gate of Hollings Prison, I noticed that there was a larger-than-usual crowd of anti-death penalty protestors. I was going to see my client who was scheduled to die by lethal injection tonight. I had mixed feelings, since I knew he was guilty as hell. But still, he was my client.

Molly had been married six times. Two of those marriages—the second and the fifth—were to the same man, so maybe you only count it as five. When they found her body, there were plenty of suspects to interview.

I had always dreamed of being a writer...

Part II

Famous First Lines

Famous First Lines

There are very few first lines of a book that are more recognizable than "In the beginning, God created the heavens and the earth" from Genesis. It's a line that almost everyone knows. Although we've offered you 101 suggested opening lines, the following are lines from famous books, some you may have read; some you might have missed while sleeping through that course in school. But they all have one thing in common — they grab your interest and welcome you into the book. Read through them and see how the author has used this first line to entice you, to give you a hint what's coming, or to awaken your emotions.

A squat grey building of only thirty-four stories.
~Aldous Huxley
Brave New World (1932)

A story has no beginning or end; arbitrarily one chooses that moment of experience from which to look back or from which to look ahead.
~Graham Greene
The End of the Affair (1951)

ABANDON ALL HOPE YE WHO ENTER HERE is scrawled in blood red lettering on the side of the Chemical Bank near the Corner of Eleventh and First and is in print large enough to be seen from the backseat of the cab as it lurches forward in the traffic leaving Wall Street and just as Timothy Price notices the words a bus pulls up, the advertisement for Les Miserables on its side blocking his view, but Price

who is with Pierce & Pierce and twenty-six doesn't seem to care because he tells the driver he will give him five dollars to turn up the radio, "Be My Baby" on WYNN, and the driver, black, not American, does so.
~Bret Easton Ellis
American Psycho (1991)

Alice was beginning to get very tired of sitting by her sister on the riverbank, and of having nothing to do: once or twice she had peeped into the book her sister was reading, but it had no pictures or conversations in it, 'and what is the use of a book,' thought Alice, 'without pictures or conversation?'
~Lewis Carroll
Alice's Adventures in Wonderland (1865)

All happy families are alike; each unhappy family is unhappy in its own way.
~Leo Tolstoy
Anna Karenina (1877)

All this happened, more or less.
~Kurt Vonnegut
Slaughterhouse-Five (1969)

As Gregor Samsa awoke from a night of uneasy dreaming, he found himself transformed in his bed into a gigantic insect.
~Franz Kafka
The Metamorphosis (1915)

Bang! Bang! Bang! Bang! Four shots ripped into my groin and I was off on the greatest adventure of my life!

~Max Shulman
Sleep Till Noon (1967)

Call me Ishmael.

~Herman Melville
Moby-Dick (1851)

Elmer Gantry was drunk.

~Sinclair Lewis
Elmer Gantry (1927)

He was an inch, perhaps two, under six feet, powerfully built, and he advanced straight at you with a slight stoop of his shoulders, head forward, and a fixed from-under stare which made you think of a charging bull.

~Joseph Conrad
Lord Jim (1900)

He was an old man who fished alone in a skiff in the Gulf Stream and he had gone eighty-four days now without taking a fish.

~Ernest Hemingway
The Old Man and the Sea (1952)

I am a sick man. . . I am a spiteful man.

~Fyodor Dostoyevsky
Notes from Underground (1864; trans. Michael R. Katz)

I am an American, Chicago born—Chicago, that somber city—and go at things as I have taught myself, and will make the record in my own way: first to knock, first admitted; sometimes an innocent knock, sometimes a not so innocent.
~Saul Bellow
The Adventures of Augie March (1953)

I am an invisible man.
~Ralph Ellison
Invisible Man (1952)

I had the story, bit by bit, from various people, and, as generally happens in such cases, each time it was a different story.
~Edith Wharton
Ethan Frome (1911)

I have never begun a novel with more misgiving.
~W. Somerset Maugham
The Razor's Edge (1944)

I was born in the Year of 1632, at the City of York, of a good Family, tho' not of that Country, my Father being a Foreigner of Bremen, who settled first at Hull; He got a good Estate by Merchandise, and leaving off his Trade, lived afterward at York, from whence he had married my Mother, whose Relations were named Robinson, a very good Family in that Country, and from whom I was called Robinson

Kreutznaer; but by the usual Corruption of Words in England, we are now called, nay we call ourselves, and write our Name Crusoe, and so my Companions always call'd me.

~Daniel Defoe
Robinson Crusoe (1719)

If I am out of my mind, it's all right with me, thought Moses Herzog.

~Saul Bellow
Herzog (1963)

If you really want to hear about it, the first thing you'll probably want to know is where I was born, and what my lousy childhood was like, and how my parents were occupied and all before they had me, and all that David Copperfield kind of crap, but I don't feel like going into it, if you want to know the truth.

~J. D. Salinger
The Catcher in the Rye (1951)

In a hole in the ground there lived a hobbit.

~J. R. R. Tolkien
The Hobbit (1937)

In a sense, I am Jacob Horner.

~John Barth
The End of the Road (1958)

In my younger and more vulnerable years my father gave me some advice that I've been turning over in my mind ever since.
~F. Scott Fitzgerald
The Great Gatsby (1925)

In the late summer of that year we lived in a house in a village that looked across the river and the plain to the mountains.
~Ernest Hemingway
A Farewell to Arms (1929)

In the town, there were two mutes and they were always together.
~Carson McCullers
The Heart is a Lonely Hunter (1940)

It is a truth universally acknowledged, that a single man in possession of a good fortune, must be in want of a wife.
~Jane Austen
Pride and Prejudice (1813)

It was a bright cold day in April, and the clocks were striking thirteen.
~George Orwell
1984 (1949)

It was a dark and stormy night, the rain fell in torrents, except at occasional intervals, when it was

checked by a violent gust of wind which swept by the streets (for it is in London that our scene lies), rattling along the house-tops, and fiercely agitating the scanty flame of the lamps that struggled against the darkness.
~Edward George Bulwer-Lytton
Paul Cllifford (1830)

It was a pleasure to burn.
~Ray Bradbury
Fahrenheit 451 (1953)

It was a queer, sultry summer, the summer they electrocuted the Rosenbergs, and I didn't know what I was doing in New York.
~Sylvia Plath
The Bell Jar (1963)

It was about eleven o'clock in the morning, mid October, with the sun not shining and a look of hard wet rain in the clearness of the foothills.
~Raymond Chandler
The Big Sleep (1939)

It was just noon that Sunday morning when the sheriff reached the jail with Lucas Beauchamp though the whole town (the whole county too for that matter) had known since the night before that Lucas had killed a white man.
~William Faulkner,
Intruder in the Dust (1948)

It was love at first sight.
>~Joseph Heller
>*Catch-22* (1961)

It was the best of times, it was the worst of times, it was the age of wisdom, it was the age of foolishness, it was the epoch of belief, it was the epoch of incredulity, it was the season of Light, it was the season of Darkness, it was the spring of hope, it was the winter of despair.
>~Charles Dickens
>*A Tale of Two Cities* (1859)

Like the brief doomed flare of exploding suns that registers dimly on blind men's eyes, the beginning of the horror passed almost unnoticed; in the shriek of what followed, in fact, was forgotten and perhaps not connected to the horror at all.
>~William Peter Blatty
>*The Exorcist* (1971)

Lolita, light of my life, fire of my loins.
>~Vladimir Nabokov
>*Lolita* (1955)

Many years later, as he faced the firing squad, Colonel Aureliano Buendia was to remember that distant afternoon when his father took him to discover ice.
>~Gabriel Garcia Márquez
>*One Hundred Years of Solitude* (1967)

Marley was dead, to begin with.
>~Charles Dickens
>*A Christmas Carol* (1843)

Mother died today.
>~Albert Camus
>*The Stranger* (1942; trans. Stuart Gilbert)

Mr and Mrs Dursley, of number four Privet Drive, were proud to say that they were perfectly normal, thank you very much.
>~J. K. Rowling
>*Harry Potter and the Sorcerer's Stone* (1998)

Mr Sherlock Holmes, who was usually very late in the mornings, save upon those not infrequent occasions when he stayed up all night, was seated at the breakfast table.
>~Arthur Conan Doyle
>*The Hound of the Baskervilles* (1901)

No one would have believed, in the last years of the nineteenth century, that this world was being watched keenly and closely by intelligences greater than man's and yet as mortal as his own; that as men busied themselves about their various concerns, they were being scrutinized and studied, perhaps almost as narrowly asas a man with a microscope might scrutinize the transient creatures that swarm and multiply in a drop of water.
>~H. G. Wells
>*The War of the Worlds* (1898)

Of all the things that drive men to sea, the most common disaster, I've come to learn, is women.
~Charles Johnson
Middle Passage (1990)

Once upon a time and a very good time it was there was a moocow coming down along the road and this moocow that was coming down along the road met a nicens little boy named baby tuckoo.
~James Joyce
A Portrait of the Artist as a Young Man (1916)

Once upon a time when the world was young there was a Martian named Smith. Valentine Michael Smith was as real as taxes but he was a race of one.
~Robert Heinlein
Stranger in a Strange Land (1961)

Once upon a time, there was a woman who discovered she had turned into the wrong person.
~Anne Tyler
Back When We Were Grownups (2001)

Somewhere in la Mancha, in a place whose name I do not care to remember, a gentleman lived not long ago, one of those who has a lance and ancient shield on a shelf and keeps a skinny nag and a greyhound for racing.
~Miguel de Cervantes
Don Quixote (1695; trans. Edith Grossman)

The cold passed reluctantly from the earth, and the retiring fogs revealed an army stretched out on the hills, resting.

~Stephen Crane
The Red Badge of Courage (1895)

The towers of Zenith aspired above the morning mist; austere towers of steel and cement and limestone, sturdy as cliffs and delicate as silver rods.

~Sinclair Lewis
Babbitt (1922)

They shoot the white girl first.

~Toni Morrison
Paradise (1998)

Through the fence, between the curling flower spaces, I could see them hitting.

~William Faulkner
The Sound and the Fury (1929)

"To be born again," sang Gibreel Farishta tumbling from the heavens, "first you have to die."

~Salman Rushdie
The Satanic Verses (1988)

To the red country and part of the gray country of Oklahoma, the last rains came gently, and they did not cut the scarred earth.

~John Steinbeck
The Grapes of Wrath (1939)

True!—nervous—very, very nervous I had been and am; but why will you say that I am mad?
~Edgar Allan Poe
The Tell-Tale Heart (1843)

Vaughan died yesterday in his last car-crash.
~J. G. Ballard
Crash (1973)

When he was nearly thirteen, my brother Jem got his arm badly broken at the elbow.
~Harper Lee
To Kill a Mockingbird (1960)

Whether I shall turn out to be the hero of my own life, or whether that station will be held by anybody else, these pages must show.
~Charles Dickens
David Copperfield (1850)

You better not never tell nobody but God.
~Alice Walker
The Color Purple (1982)

You don't know about me without you have read a book by the name of The Adventures of Tom Sawyer; but that ain't no matter.
~Mark Twain
Adventures of Huckleberry Finn (1855)

Dear Reader (Writer?)

We hope you enjoyed this book and that it's helped stimulate some creative ideas in you. You're welcome to use any of these lines in your forthcoming novel or short story, but keep in mind that there are only 101 suggestions and if we sell more than 101 copies of this book, it's entirely possible someone else will be starting his or her next book with the same line as yours.

We are planning to publish a second volume of "The Writer's Block Survival Guide," and we would love to receive your suggested first lines. If you would like to contribute (with attribution, of course) your ideas, please fill in the lines below and mail it to us. When we reach our magic number of 101 First Lines (don't ask, it just seems like a good number), we will put together our next edition.

Cut out this page and mail it to us at:

Webster House Publishing LLC
P.O. Box 294
Georgetown, CT 06829

_____

_____

_____

_____

Name (please print)_____
Email_____

Please use the following pages to write your own additional first lines, story ideas, dialogues, and any other notes that will help you on the road to writing your Great American Novel.

www.ingramcontent.com/pod-product-compliance
Lightning Source LLC
Chambersburg PA
CBHW061446040426
42450CB00007B/1241